GOD SAID IT
THE LIFE OF MOSES

BRADLEY BOOTH

Nampa, Idaho | www.pacificpress.com

Cover design by Gerald Lee Monks
Cover design resources from Marcus Mashburn
Inside design by Gerald Lee Monks
Inside illustrations by Marcus Mashburn

Copyright © 2019 by Pacific Press® Publishing Association
Printed in the United States of America
All rights reserved

The author assumes full responsibility for the accuracy of all facts and quotations as cited in this book.

Scripture quotations marked NKJV are from New King James Version®. Copyright © 1982 by Thomas Nelson. Used by permission. All rights reserved.

You can obtain additional copies of this book by calling toll-free 1-800-765-6955 or by visiting AdventistBookCenter.com.

Library of Congress Cataloging-in-Publication Data

Names: Booth, Bradley, 1957– author.
Title: God said it #3 : the life of Moses / Bradley Booth.
Other titles: God said it number 3 | Life of Moses
Description: Nampa : Pacific Press Publishing Association, 2018.
Identifiers: LCCN 2018054887 | ISBN 9780816364824 (pbk. : alk. paper)
Subjects: LCSH: Moses (Biblical leader)—Juvenile literature. | Bible stories, English.
Classification: LCC BS580.M6 B66 2018 | DDC 222/.1092—dc23 LC record available at https://lccn.loc.gov/2018054887

July 2019

CONTENTS

Introduction 5

Chapter 1: Baby Moses 7

Chapter 2: Moses and the Burning Bush 13

Chapter 3: Moses and the Ten Plagues 19

Chapter 4: Moses and the Ten Commandments 25

COLORING PAGES

Check out the coloring pages in the middle of this book. They are based on the featured stories and are meant to be colored in by the reader and presented as a gift to a person they appreciate. These may include

- parents,
- sisters or brothers,
- grandparents,
- aunts and uncles,
- teachers,
- neighbors, or
- friends.

INTRODUCTION

God Said It introduces children to the Bible. It is designed to help children understand the importance of reading and learning from the Word of God. Our prayer is that parents, teachers, church visitors, and mentors of children everywhere use this book to reach young people for Jesus.

The Scriptures contain hundreds of stories about people who trusted and obeyed God, people getting to know God, and people choosing to go their own way. In the stories of Moses as a baby, at the burning bush, during the ten plagues, and receiving the Ten Commandments, kids can learn that God has a good plan for everyone who follows Him.

God Said It is dedicated to God's faithful witnesses in the Bible and to all the boys and girls who read these stories. We trust that the stories on these pages will draw children to Jesus. May they choose to be faithful like the Bible heroes from long ago so that they can one day shine "like the stars forever" (Daniel 12:3, NKJV).

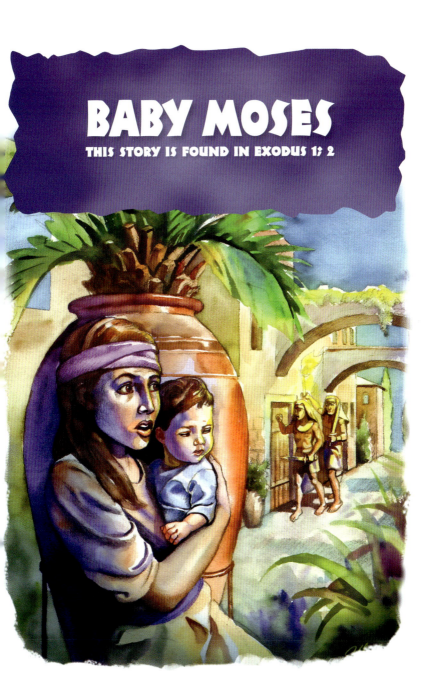

Baby Moses was born into a family of slaves in ancient Egypt. In those days, being a baby boy was very dangerous because Pharaoh had ordered that all Hebrew baby boys had to be thrown into the Nile River.

"The Hebrew population is growing too fast," Pharaoh said. "If they should someday decide to start a war against Egypt, we would lose for sure. There are too many of them."

And so it was that the Egyptians were ordered to go from house to house to kill the babies. It was a very scary time for Moses' family because he was just a newborn. His mother, Jochebed, tried to keep him quiet so that no one would know there was a baby in her home. However, by the time Moses was three months old, she knew it was no longer possible to keep him hidden.

To save him from Pharaoh's soldiers, she decided to do something very unusual. Bringing some reeds up from the marshes of the Nile River, she made a little basket boat and a lid for it. Then she swabbed some sticky pitch on the outside to keep it watertight. Finally, she put little Moses in the basket and knelt with her family to pray for his safety.

At dawn, she carried the basket down to the river's edge and put it among the reeds near the place where the royal family went to bathe each morning. Moses' older sister, Miriam, hid among the reeds to watch and see what would happen. Perhaps the princess and her attendants would find him and have compassion for him.

And that's exactly what happened. When the princess came for her usual morning bath along the river, she saw the basket among the reeds. Quick as a wink, she sent one of her maids to fetch it.

To her delight, she found a little Hebrew baby inside, and he was crying. The princess felt compassion for this baby. It was clear that his mother had put him there to save him from being destroyed by the Egyptians.

Immediately, she decided to take the baby home and adopt him as her own. This would mean he would grow up in the royal palace and be educated by royal priests and teachers.

But for now, she needed someone to take care of the baby for her, and just at that moment, Miriam came out of hiding. "Would you like for me to find someone to care for the baby?" she asked.

"Yes, that would be wonderful," the princess said. "Thank you."

Miriam ran home to tell her mother the good news, and soon they were back at the river.

"Please take care of this little baby for me," the princess said, "and I will pay you wages."

What an answer to prayer! Baby Moses would now be safe, and he could be raised by his own mother.

Jochebed knew she would not have little Moses forever, so she made the best use of her time with him. Every morning she told him stories about God and His care for His people. Every day she taught him songs of praise that would help him be faithful to the God of Abraham, Isaac, and Jacob. Every night she taught him to pray to the God of heaven, who would one day save their people from slavery.

Jochebed knew God had a very special plan for Moses' life. She could not know that Moses would one day lead the Hebrews out of Egypt to the land of Canaan, but she was sure God had kept her baby safe for a reason. And for now, that was enough. You can read all about it in the Bible.

MOSES AND THE BURNING BUSH

THIS STORY IS FOUND IN EXODUS 2-5

oses was the son of Hebrew slaves, but when he was about twelve years old, he went to live in the palace with Pharaoh's daughter, the princess. He attended Egyptian schools, ate Egyptian food, and wore Egyptian clothes. The Egyptians worshiped pagan idols that represented animal gods, such as snakes and dogs, or the sun god, but Moses would not join them. He chose to be faithful to the worship of Jehovah, the Creator of heaven and earth, as his mother had taught him.

By the time he was forty years old, Moses was the crown prince and the favorite of everyone. He could have been the next pharaoh and freed the Hebrews from slavery, but something happened to change all that. One day he saw an Egyptian taskmaster beating a Hebrew slave. He got very angry with the taskmaster, and when Moses tried to stop him, he killed the Egyptian.

Moses knew he was in trouble for what he had done, so he fled to the desert. He wandered for days until he came to an oasis in the land of Midian. While there, he met seven sisters who had brought their sheep to the well for water but were being bullied by other shepherds. Moses chased the mean shepherds away, and for his kindness, he was invited to eat with Jethro, the girls' father. Jethro invited Moses to stay with him, and it wasn't long before Moses married Jethro's oldest daughter, Zipporah.

Years passed as Moses tended sheep in the mountains of Midian. He knew he had spoiled God's plan for

him to help free the Hebrews, but he couldn't change that now. He was a fugitive in the land of Midian.

One day as he was walking with his sheep through the hills, he noticed something very strange. A bush was on fire, but it wasn't burning up. It burned and burned, and when he drew near the bush to get a closer look, he heard a voice.

BABY MOSES
EXODUS 1; 2

This is a gift for _____.

From _____

MOSES AND THE BURNING BUSH
EXODUS 2-5

This is a gift for _____.

From _____

MOSES AND THE TEN PLAGUES
EXODUS 5-12

This is a gift for _____.

From _____

MOSES AND THE TEN COMMANDMENTS
EXODUS 14; 19; 20

This is a gift for _____.

From _____

"Take the sandals off your feet," the voice said, "for you are standing on holy ground. I am the God of Abraham, Isaac, and Jacob."

Moses quickly bowed his face to the ground with reverence as he realized he was in the very presence of God.

"I have seen how My people are suffering in slavery," God said. "I want you to go back to Egypt to bring the Hebrews out of slavery. It's time to take them to the Promised Land in Canaan."

"I can't do the job," Moses said. "I'm a nobody. No one will believe me or listen to me."

"Don't worry; I will be with you," God insisted. "I will give you the power to do amazing miracles so that everyone will know I sent you. However, when you ask Pharaoh to let the Hebrews go free, he won't do it. For that, I will send many plagues of judgment on Egypt."

Moses was still unsure, so God performed two incredible miracles to convince him.

"Throw your shepherd's rod on the ground," He told Moses, and wonder of wonders, when Moses threw down his rod, the stick became a snake.

Then God told him to pick up the snake by the tail, and when he did, it became a rod again. Moses had never seen anything so amazing in all his life, but God wasn't done.

"Put your hand inside the folds of your mantle," the Lord said, "and then pull it out again."

Moses obeyed, and with horror, he saw that his hand had turned as white as snow. He had leprosy, but when he put his hand back inside the mantle, the leprosy disappeared.

It was all so amazing, but Moses still doubted that he could carry out the mission. "I haven't been in Egypt for years!" he complained. "I don't even know the language that well anymore."

"Stop arguing!" God told Moses. "Your brother will go with you. He knows the language well." That settled it, and Moses finally agreed to go.

Now the pharaoh was in for a big surprise. He would be stubborn and refuse to let the Hebrews go free, but God would teach him some lessons. That's another great story in your Bible.

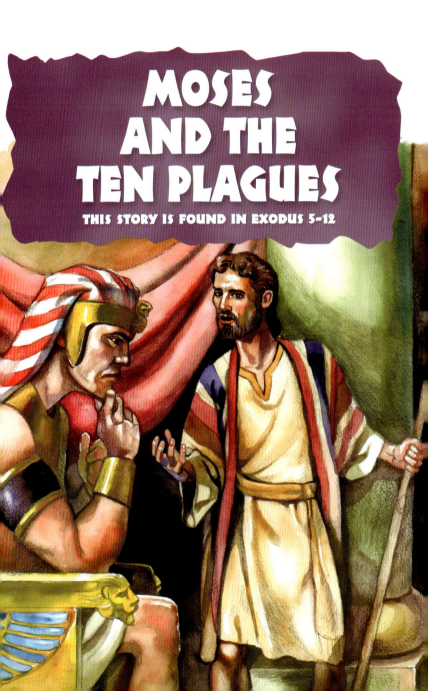

Moses and Aaron stood in the courtroom of the Egyptian palace. Shiny floors of marble gleamed white in the morning light. Exotic plants and golden furniture sat along the walls. Armored guards stood with shining swords and shields.

"Jehovah, the God of Israel, commands that you let His people go free," Aaron told the pharaoh.

"Who is this God of the Hebrew slaves that I should obey Him?" Pharaoh asked. "I don't know Jehovah, and I won't let Israel go either. If you think the slaves need to worship, they must be lazy," he added. "From now on, they can gather their own straw to make the bricks."

This additional work made the slaves very upset, but Moses told them not to worry. "Jehovah will punish Pharaoh with terrible plagues for his cruelty," he said.

The next morning, Moses stretched his rod over the Nile River. Suddenly the river turned to blood. All the fish in the river died, and that made the water stink, plus there was no water to drink.

Pharaoh didn't seem to care, so God sent a plague of frogs. Thousands of them! They were hopping everywhere, getting into the houses and food and even the beds. These first two plagues were very hard for the Egyptians because they worshiped the Nile River and frogs as gods.

Finally, Pharaoh couldn't stand the frogs any longer. "Ask your God to take away the frogs, and I'll let the

slaves go worship Jehovah," he said.

The frogs died, and that made Egypt stink even more. But Pharaoh didn't keep his promise, so God sent a plague of mosquito gnats. These tiny insects drove the Egyptians crazy with their bites, and still, Pharaoh wouldn't let the slaves go free. So God sent swarms of flies.

The Hebrew slaves had suffered from the effects of the first three plagues, but this fourth plague was different. The flies came only to the homes and palaces of the Egyptians, and they bit the people viciously, making everyone sick.

Pharaoh promised to let the slaves go free if Moses would remove the flies. However, when the flies disappeared, the proud king changed his mind once again.

So God sent a disease throughout the land of Egypt. Not surprisingly, cattle, goats, camels, and donkeys died by the thousands. However, the livestock of the Hebrews did not suffer from the disease, and still, Pharaoh would not set the slaves free.

Next came a plague of disease on all the Egyptians. The disease made people get painful sores all over their bodies, but Pharaoh still would not change his mind and let the Israelite slaves go.

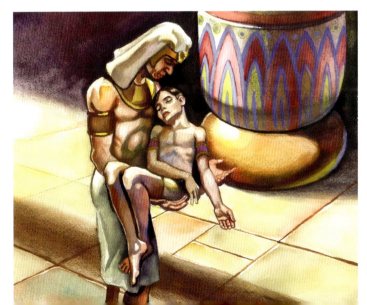

Next came a terrible thunderstorm, with lightning and giant hailstones that rained down from the sky. The storm killed all the livestock and people in the fields and flattened all the crops.

In the next plague, hordes of grasshoppers swarmed over the land of Egypt and ate everything the storm had left behind. Pharaoh begged for God's mercy, but he still would not let the slaves go free.

Darkness came to Egypt in the ninth plague, and no one could see anything, day or night. The plague lasted three days, and it was hard for people even to breathe. However, as with the plagues of flies, disease, storms, and grasshoppers, the plague of darkness only came to the Egyptians.

Pharaoh pleaded for mercy once again but then changed his mind, and that brought the tenth and final plague. Every firstborn child in Egypt died during the night before the Hebrew slaves left Egypt. Only the Hebrews were spared because they put the blood of a lamb on the doorposts of their homes. God had told them to do this to show that Jesus' death would one day save them from their sins.

When Pharaoh saw that his own son was dead, he finally set the Hebrews free. What a shame that God had to destroy nearly everything in Egypt to get him to do it! Pharaoh learned too late that it never pays to disobey God. The Lord says what He means and means what He says.

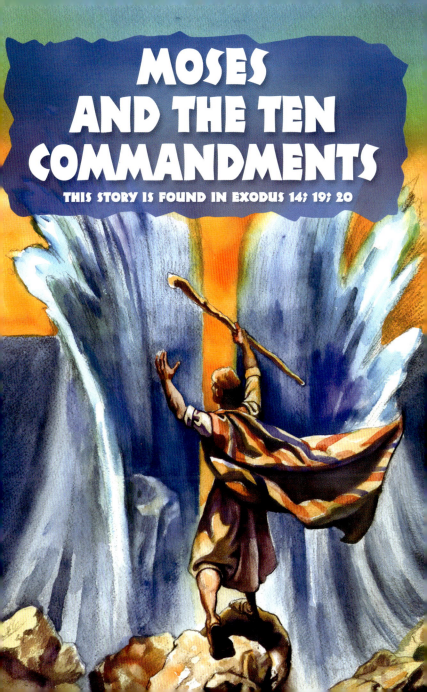

Moses was one of the coolest leaders in the history of God's people. He could have been king on a throne in the land of the pyramids; but instead he chose to follow God—who used Moses' decision to work out His plan to set the Hebrews free. To do this, God sent ten terrible plagues on Egypt. Then, with Egypt in shambles, there was nothing to stop the Hebrews from leaving for Canaan.

Nothing, that is, but hot winds and desert sands. The Hebrews didn't have much food, and even less water, and when they reached the Red Sea, their problems really started.

Suddenly everyone noticed clouds of dust in the west and realized that Pharaoh and his army were coming to take them captive. They didn't want to be slaves again and begged Moses to save them!

And then God did another incredible miracle for His people. He opened a path through the Red Sea so that the Hebrews could cross over to the other side. That's right! Moses held his shepherd's rod over the water, and the sea parted right down the middle. Wow! How neat was that?

The people excitedly grabbed up their belongings and headed through the pathway in the sea. All night they hurried, and by dawn, they were safely on the other side.

Unfortunately, Pharaoh's army came right after them through the sea. However, God was watching out

for the Hebrews, and now He reversed this amazing miracle. In a moment, He allowed the walls of water to come crashing down on the terrified Egyptian soldiers.

With praises to God, the Hebrews traveled on through the desert until they reached Mount Sinai.

It was here that the most famous meeting ever held between God and His people took place.

On a very special day, God came down to the mountain and gave the Hebrews His Ten Commandments. In a blaze of thunder and fire, He spoke the commandments and wrote them with His own finger on slabs of stone.

Commandment 1 said we are not to have any other gods, and commandment 2 said we should never make idols of these gods. Commandment 3 tells us never to use God's name lightly. Commandment 4 reminds us to keep the seventh day of each week holy as God's Sabbath. This is a memorial reminding people that God created the earth in six days and rested on the seventh.

Commandment 5 tells us to honor our parents, to be kind to them and care for them. Commandments 6 through 10 tell us not to murder, to be faithful and true to our husband or wife, not to steal or lie, and never to be jealous of the things other people have.

These commandments are God's ten most important rules for us. If we love Him, we will obey them.

God didn't invent the Ten Commandments that day on Mount Sinai. His law has always existed—even in heaven before He created this world. His commandments are an expression of His character, of who He is and how much He cares about us. God is loving, and that is exactly what His law is all about.

When God wrote the commandments on slabs of

stone, He gave them to Moses, who later put them inside the sacred ark of God's covenant. This ark was kept in the Most Holy Place of God's wilderness tabernacle and went with the Hebrews on their travels in the desert.

When the Hebrews finally entered the land of Canaan, Moses did not get to go with them as he had hoped. He died before they crossed the Jordan River, but God rewarded him for his faithfulness and raised him to life a short time later in a special resurrection.

Moses is in heaven now. He can read God's original Ten Commandments any time he wants because they are in the heavenly sanctuary. We can be sure those commandments remind Moses of that day so long ago when God made a copy of them for the Hebrews. What an amazing story from the Bible!

Want to know more about what God said?

It's easy with FREE eBooklets & Bible Guides just for you!

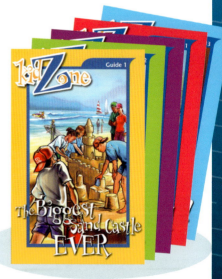

1. Go to **kidsvop.com**
2. Click on Bible Guides
3. Get started!

To receive KidZone in print, go to
KidsBibleinfo.com/request

Your parents can also learn more about what God says at **Bibleinfo.com**

voice of prophecy